Floppy odd one out

join up the same and colour

join up the same and colour

join up

join up

colour the round things ○ ○ ○

make the same

Biff → Biff

make the same

Chip → Chip

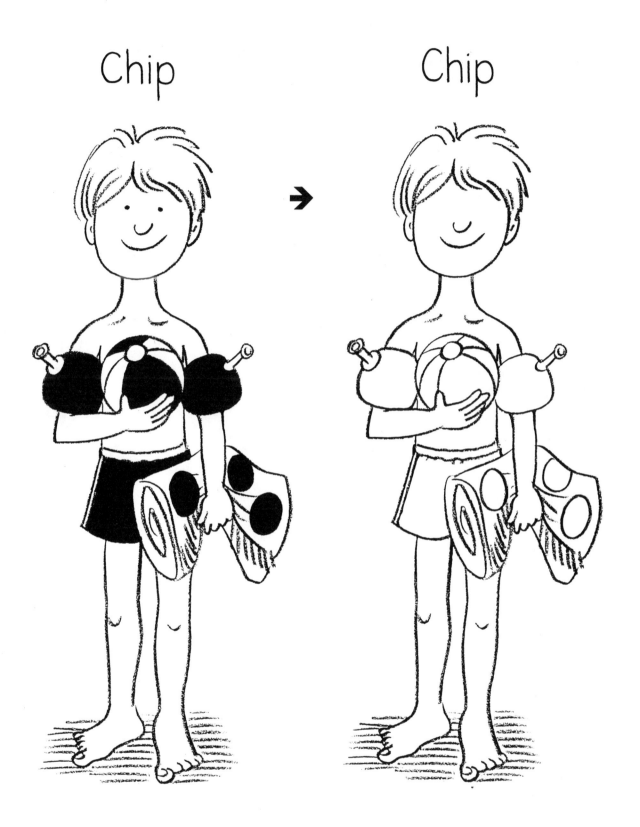

what comes next?

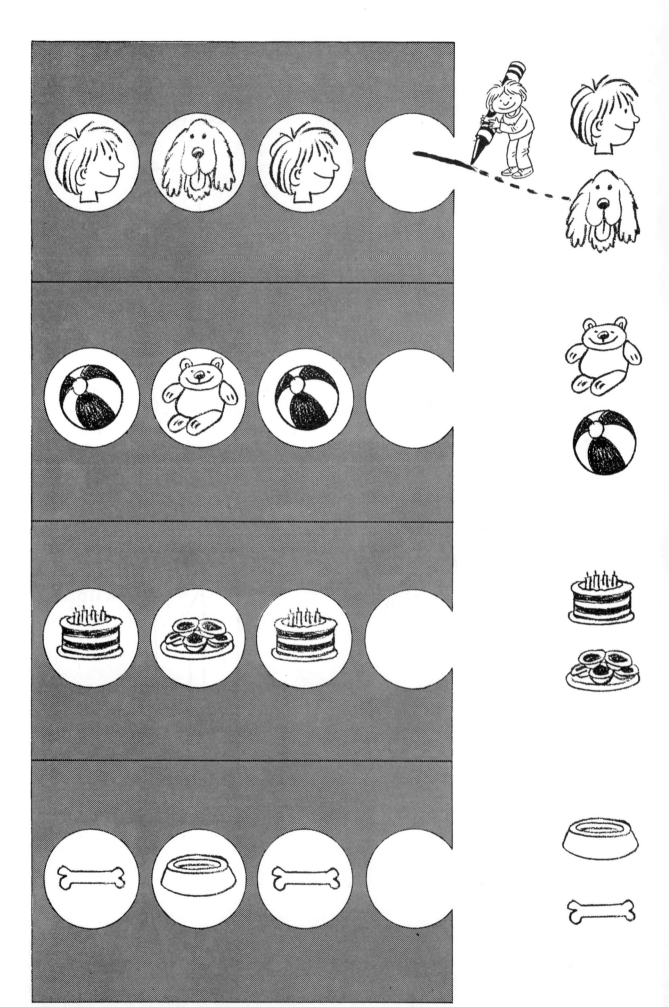

what comes next?

what happens next?

what happens next?

© Oxford University Press 1986
Printed in Hong Kong
Pictures by Alex Brychta

Available in packs
ISBN 0 19 916074 0 (pack of six)
ISBN 0 19 916238 7 (class pack of thirty)

First published 1986
Reprinted 1986, 1987, 1989, 1990, 199
1992, 1993

name

Kipper Colour

Kipper odd one out